PRAISE FOR THE REPUBLIC OF VENICE

Poggio Bracciolini

Translated by: D.P. Curtin

Dalcassian Publishing Company

PHILADELPHIA, PA

PRAISE FOR THE REPUBLIC OF VENICE

Copyright @ 2007 Dalcassian Publishing Company

All rights reserved. No part of this publication may be reproduced, distributed, or transmitted in any form or by any means, including photocopying, recording, or other electronic or mechanical methods, without the prior written permission of the publisher, except in the case of brief quotations embodied in critical reviews and certain other non-commercial uses permitted by copyright law. For permission request, write to Dalcassian Publishing Company at dalcassianpublishing at gmail.com

ISBN: 979-8-8692-4143-6 (Paperback)

Library of Congress Control Number:
Author: Curtin, D.P. (1985-)

Printed by Ingram Content Group, 1 Ingram Blvd, La Vergne, Tennessee

First printing edition 2007.

PRAISE FOR THE REPUBLIC OF VENICE

PRAISE FOR THE REPUBLIC OF VENICE

THE SPEECH OF POGIUS OF FLORENCE IN PRAISE OF THE REPUBLIC OF THE VENETIANS.

1. Desiring to pursue the singular excellence of the republic of Venice in all kinds of virtues, with which I could praise them, and for the most part to this day they diverted me from the pursuit of writing, and from domestic affairs, and some fear that I should not be able to perform the eloquence of speaking in proportion to the dignity of things. But now, relying on greater leisure, and at the same time turning to the mind that the strong are wont to be helped by fortune, I decided to explain in letters what I had previously conceived in my mind, so that so excellent a city would be celebrated by our praises for its merits, and the rest of the institutions of the republic, which had been so well established, would be inspired by their memory and praise. For if at any time there has ever been a republic worthy of praise and glory, if at any time it has obeyed the precepts of justice, if it has used good morals to maintain gravity and dignity both in private and in public affairs, if any has existed in which the common advantage has been preferred to private advantage, this is indeed the one which meritoriously precedes the glory of all that is, that was, and that which is to come.

2. There are various kinds of polities, according to what Aristotle likes, two of which he prefers to the rest, the kingdom of the silicate and the aristocracy, which ours call the nobility, and which Cicero in his books *De Legibus* says is the best, when the best men, as it pleases him, govern, praise and glory servants, preservers of the country and lovers of the republic. I can truly assert that there never was such a thing among the Venetians, among whom only the nobles govern the city, obeying the laws, and intending all to the benefit of the public state, putting aside all private concerns. Aristotle never saw or read that this aristocracy never existed. For if he had been able to observe it anywhere, in which the prince, as the head, presides over the rest in dignity, and is himself the parent of the laws, and then the nobles, as members adhering to the head, follow justice as a certain driver in their actions, he would undoubtedly have preferred this to all the rest. For he saw in it as if the image of a king, and the nobles afterwards with one mind, with one voice, conspiring in one and the same opinion, and that the kingdom and the aristocracy were contained in the same republic. From which it is necessary to arbitrate that it is the best republic of all. Aristotle himself admits that it is better to have many goods than to have one king. And so, it seems that it is so much better for a kingdom to be overcome by an aristocratic republic, inasmuch as it is greater, more plentiful, more extensive, more fruitful, and in use the virtue of many is better than that of one. This is also the opinion of Lampridius in the Life of Alexander Severus. For he said: It is well known to your piety, which you read in Marius Maximus, that a republic is better and almost safer in which there is an evil prince than in that in which the friends of the evil prince are. Indeed, one evil can be corrected by many goods, but many evils cannot be overcome by one, however good, in any way. What kind of state, then, is that republic to be called, which adds the best advisers to a good prince, and contracts the strength of many into one will? She is indeed to be considered the most blessed and the most excellent of all, and whom Aristotle never knew. I also think that Plato, if he had been able to see this excellent form of governing the state, would have set no other model in his work. For he sought the best state of the republic, the foundation of which he designated justice, that it should be accompanied by reward and punishment, so that the good men of virtue would be encouraged to praise by the reward, while the bad would be deterred from evil by the purposeful execution of their crimes. It is necessary that this should be what the philosophers sought, by whose precepts that republic was established, in which

justice reigns overall, by which the good are honored for their merits, and the reprobate are affected with due notice.

3. But in order that the virtue of this republic in the administration of justice may shine out more in comparison with others, let us consider the ancient polities and their manners. The Lacedaemonians are especially praised, who are said to have lived for nearly seven hundred years with only laws and never changing customs. But in them the varying condition of being always governed, and the state never longer remaining in the same state, and now subject to kings, now to tyrants, now torn by various factions, now shaken by internal discords, clearly shows that it is not happy but most unhappy, not quiet but turbulent, not in the interests of the public, but that she was devoted to private hatreds, and finally, after many defeats by the Romans, she underwent slavery.

4. Greek history testifies to the fact that the Athenian city was used as a republic. The judgment of the people was about every matter, and that which was done with the knowledge of the people was considered fair and firm. The best and most distinguished men were expelled from the city by the onslaught of the multitude excited by these decrees. Eminent citizens were condemned by the judgment of the people. Great emperors or extortionists were punished by exile or imprisonment. Now at the service of kings, now at the cruelty of tyrants, now agitated by the rashness of the people, a most ungrateful city indeed, which, as a reward for things well done, afflicted its warlords with various calamities, always agitated either by domestic seditions or foreign wars. The wicked were preferred to the good, and the wicked were added to the offices of the republic. And so their liberty was lost.

5. The city of the Thebans failed with a similar destruction. Now submitting to more powerful citizens, now to tyrants, now harassed by domestic factions, so that you may say that there was no republic in it, but the rashness of contentions.

6. They bear a great and insolent republic of the Carthaginians, which for nearly forty years contended with the Roman people for dominion. But we read how variously, how cruelly, how barbarously, how savagely it was administered: certainly, it inflicted the most excellent men on its emperors either with the most cruel death, or proscribed it, so that it would rather be called a proud and impotent tyrant than a republic.

7. The Roman republic was the greatest of all that ever existed, and was celebrated with the highest praise. Eloquence and eloquence either won or

equaled them all. He overcame the military force. Many of the best and most illustrious men flourished in it in every kind of praise. But who does not know how many and how many new movements in that city from the very beginning of liberty, how many varieties of things, how many whirlwinds, how many dissensions, dissensions, and seditions have prevailed among the mobile people, how many and how many struggles of the country and the people have been stirred up, what discussions of fathers and consuls with the tribunes of the people? feuds, hatreds, more than civil wars, thefts, robberies, excommunications of citizens, exiles of the best men, and finally innumerable tumults arose, or when the stormy sea was tossed with continuous waves. I do not enumerate the spoils, sacrileges, rapes, murders, desolation of cities, the lust and avarice of soldiers. I will pass over the worst tyranny over the subjects, the heinous crimes committed in the provinces by the strange lust of the ancestors. Cicero himself testifies that more allied cities were destroyed by the winter soldiers than enemy cities by their weapons. I am silent about the various conspiracies raised against the republic, and the whole world yielded to the avarice of the Romans. What shall I say of Verres, Clodius, Catilina, and others who conspired in the ruin of the provinces and the city? It seems to me that we can say this very truly: for many centuries it could not have been called a republic, but a nefarious robbery and a most cruel tyranny, when neither the laws, nor the customs and institutions of the ancients, nor the courts were valid, but force, iron, and yielding were engaged in the conspiracy of the tribunes in the forum and in the temples of the gods. Cicero himself complains that there is no republic, no courts, no senate, but at the behest of Pompey everything is done in the opposite way. Among the ancient Romans there was at one time a time when it deserved to be called a republic, but then also the secession of the people, the lust of the deceums, the exiles of Coriolan and Cammilus can be recorded.

8. But in truth the republic of Venice, being far removed from the custom of their predecessors, shunned all these vices and atrocities to which the other states and republics fell. There was no discord among them in the administration of the republic, no dissension, no contentions of the citizens, no factions, no similitudes, no open hatreds. Each one feels the same, and they all work together with one mind for the salvation of the republic. Toward this mind they direct, and to preserve it they devote all their strength. They seek this, they desire this, that their republic may be as happy as possible. Although this is considered difficult in a city so large, it should by no means seem

surprising to anyone, if they review the manner of governing the city. For there are many ancient and noble families in which the government of the republic is held. No commoner is given access or place to the functions of the state. Public duties are demanded of the nobles of the sun, and of the more distinguished men from them, so that each one, as members of one and the same body, conspires together with a single will for the health and well-being of it, and thinks that it is to be cherished and nourished as if it were one's own mother. Therefore, this republic is deservedly thought to be ahead of the others in power by a long distance, the greatest proof of which is that beyond the seven hundredth year, which no other republic has happened, it has continued to this day under the same leader, magistrates, laws, institutions, and morals.

9. But among the praises of so large and so magnificent a city, the first thing which I think contributes much to the praise and glory of the city, is its location, of which it seems necessary to speak. The city of that place was built, so that, although it was surrounded by no walls, and protected by no ramparts, yet it was the most secure of all, that no machines, no instruments of war, would frighten it, no sudden attacks, no unexpected attacks of the enemy would repel it. Surrounded on all sides by the sea, he is afraid of the outsider. For it is also five miles distant from the mainland, which they sail surrounded by, as if it were a moat, so that there is nothing to be feared on that side. And it is furnished with a single port, to which the larger ships, if they are laden, are not given access, and with triremes and other vessels they seek to drive away every hostile fleet with little effort. For in the rest of the places the waters are stagnant and like swamps and are not accessible to ships. Thus, there are no cavalry raids, no hostile classes to fear. Moreover, the wall is made of heaped stones twenty miles wide, fixed with huge piles, stable, which keeps off the force of the flowing sea from the city, and makes the stagnant places quieter.

10. What is really wonderful to say, and which affords the chief adornment and ornament to the state, is that there are navies of the greatest size and magnificent equipment, to which the rest of the world is put far behind, and for the maintenance of which taxes are sure to be instituted. Among them were more than a hundred triremes at idle, ready with their armaments, so that the commerce in use might be shut up, and a great number of freighters, so that within a month, if necessary, they would seek to bring out of the harbor a ready and equipped fleet of a hundred and fifty larger ships. For the rest of the smaller ones are almost infinite in number. For there is a great number of them, which are adapted to the use necessary for riding. For all things suitable for the

sustenance of such a large city are brought abundantly from the sea, so that there is always an abundance of all things there, and no want is to be feared. A very beautiful spectacle is afforded by the many ships either coming or going, both those going to more proper places, and those sailing to Pontus and Meotidas, the marshes, and other harbors of the infidels, and those seeking Spain, Gaul, Britain, and the Morinos for the sake of trade. All these are loaded with various things when they go to give the greatest spectacle to the city. From thence to the Mediterranean places, to other regions, other provinces, by carts, every kind of trade is carried.

11. What shall I say of the most beautiful houses, the magnificent palaces, the temples built at great expense, the streets and public places, and the city filled with various artists? Why should I review the modesty of the young, the authority of the old, the gravity of the men, the dignity of the senate, which seems to be most truly evident from kings, as Cineas once said of the Romans? Why should all citizens, who bear a certain dignity before themselves, be dressed in fine clothing? What colorful and clean furniture, in the decoration of which they spend the most care? Add to this the fact that the whole city is accessible both by roads and canals, which is a great and no small advantage. For everything that pertains to subsistence is brought home in boats. But in that which they are most to be emphasized, is the size and beauty of the churches, which they adorn with various things for the worship of religion. But these things exist in common with many others. But in that they surpass the rest, the wealth of the treasure of the church of St. Mark, which is indeed the most beautiful and wonderful to look at: there is a great wealth of gold and silver, also of pearls, and of those which the common people call precious stones, which they affirm to be both exquisite and of the greatest value.

12. Since each thing is governed and accomplished by order and reason, which I proposed to say in the second place, I will enumerate the order of the magistrates themselves, to whom the care of the government of the republic is entrusted, from the beginning of the city itself to a few institutions. At the beginning of the city, the citizens created a leader for themselves, who was to preside over all as if they were the head, and to consult the interests of the public, and who himself was subject to the laws, so that when he became superior in dignity, he would be equal to the rest in obeying the laws. For if he transgresses, he does not evade punishment, but is punished by the magistrate according to the laws established. To this alone no power was granted. He is so presiding over the rest that he alone cannot decide anything that pertains to the

PRAISE FOR THE REPUBLIC OF VENICE

republic, he cannot write letters, he cannot unlock those brought, he cannot listen to anyone, he cannot answer except to the will of six men, whose advice he must adhere to. These have supreme power and are subject to the laws. Here the senate is chosen by vote, and by the judgment of the same, if need be, it is removed, but almost all die in that position. However, judgment is under way, whether he has committed something that needs more serious criticism. But in order that it may be established how much equitable and good worship is ingrained in the minds of individuals, how modestly the leaders have lived, it is said that no one in the careers of so many centuries aspired to tyranny except one who also paid the penalty for his rashness, which seems to Hercule to be surprising, since ambition is such a powerful disease in men, so much desire to dominate But the love of country overcame all their passions. He banishes all mad desires. Moreover, they know that they are the guardians of the laws, not the masters. They know that it is the duty of the state to govern together with the rest, and not to demand government.

13. This is especially to be emphasized with the greatest praise, that their laws are firm, stable, and long-lasting in regard to the interests of the republic, and are not abrogated at the will of anyone, nor are they varied from day to day, but are preserved by perpetual sanction. There are, besides those whom I have enumerated, ten men who are appointed annually from the primaries of the city, to whom the power of punishing and proscribing criminals and criminals for whatever reason has been attributed for the quality of their deeds, from whose opinion no challenge is given, nor is it right to reconsider what they have done. It is the magistrate who administers justice, by whom the cases of citizens and foreigners are dealt with, not by the bills of the papers, not by the clever interpretation of lawyers, but by equity, modesty, and reason, in which both little expense and loss of time are spent. Nor indeed do they employ any external minister in rendering law or administering justice in any way, but they themselves claim from the order of the magistrates that right of moderation, so that there are either no or rare complaints from their judgments.

14. To these are added the stewards of the church of St. Mark, as they call them, men chosen from all, of great dignity and authority, whose duty it is to protect the treasury of the church and to administer to pious uses what remains of the worship and adornment of that religion. There are also, as they say, officers of the night, whose concern is to punish minor offenses for their quality, and especially those committed at night.

15. There is, moreover, a smaller senate of two hundred men, which they call the quorates, in which all the magistrates whom I have mentioned above assemble. In this meeting the leader presides, sitting in the highest place, and after him the rest follow according to the dignity of each. There, things pertaining to the state of the commonwealth, or to war or peace, are decided by debated opinions. It is added that when the case requires the second senate of a larger number, it is given to participate with each of the nobles, as long as they are above twenty years of age. By these suffrages individual praetors and other officials are created, to whom the outer provinces, states, and towns are assigned to be governed, or some special office is imposed upon them. There is a free opportunity for all of this group, to whom this may happen, to choose and nominate whom they wish. He who is chosen from among those nominated by the vote of the senate, gives a certain salary, as the laws dictate, to the person who nominated himself. From this fact two rewards of virtue arise: first, to him who nominates a worthy magistrate, and then to the person named, if he has been appointed. Thus, there is a contest of virtue and a rivalry between citizens, not of hatred or rashness. For everyone strives to escape by such behavior to the reputation and opinion of men, to get ahead of others in votes. They are hindered neither by prayers nor by ambition, whereby access is open to the best of all to dignities. For each one thinks that he has brought praise to himself if he nominates such a person as is deemed worthy of that dignity by the judgment of the senate.

16. I remember some who were greatly fined, who were said to have interceded with prayers for a friend in giving votes. For they want men's wills to be free in public affairs, not bought by price or by prayers. For this reason they are seldom deputed to command others except those whose prowess they have known and understood. But if those who behave towards their subjects either avariciously or more cruelly than the law permits, they are severely punished. For the complaints of the oppressed are heard, and they are vindicated by the wronged. Therefore, they keep their hands clean from wrongdoing, and do as much as the laws allow, all of which look to the worship of justice.

17. With this system of living, these manners, this order, at no time after the intermission began, was the city so justly and piously governed, so equal was the power to all in their degree, so equal was the distribution of honors and honors to men, that not by human counsels, but by some divine nod, not earthly but some heavenly monarchy, such a city, seems to be governed and preserved so harmoniously by the will of the citizens. For what they think, what

they seek, what they each pay attention to, that which they think will benefit the republic. And if, as sometimes happens, when either war or peace is to be dealt with, the opinions of the citizens are various and different from one another, what the majority has decided, the rest verify and follow, and translate their opinion, even if they feel otherwise, into the opinion of another. No obstinacy of wills persists, no hatred, no unity undermines the republic. They allow themselves to be easily defeated in their opinion. Thus, the diversity of opinion was reduced to harmony. There is no agreement or conspiracy of citizens to be held back.

18. In this agreement you could say that there was one mind, one will, one mind, one plan of all. There is no private house in which the father of the family is not unsavory, no brothers, no relatives seek so common, so harmonious a private advantage, as the Venetians seek the state and dignity of their city. No one thinks of his own business in consulting but looks before his eyes to the common advantage proposed. But this is especially the highest praise to be given: if those who are to be condemned for the crime they have committed, if they are caught on the trail, they will suffer the punishments of their crimes. No intercession is given, no respite, no subterfuge, no intervention hinders the course of justice. Exiles are rarely recalled except by exact punishment. And although they are strict enforcers of justice, that is the admirable prudence of the citizens. For if anyone be deprived of the functions of the republic by his own merit, he shall either be expelled from the city, or be punished by the head. He alone who transgresses is content with punishment. They allow others of the same race, whether of the house, or their sons, or their relatives, as harmless, to be elected to the office of magistrates, to be present at councils, to come to the senate, and to exercise the functions of the republic. The father is often banished, preserving his former position in the city and the place of his son, so that, according to the prophetic opinion, the soul that has sinned may itself die. They are alone there; the state of the rest of the republic is preserved intact.

19. Nor indeed is it permissible for anyone to reprove the mistakes of another or to criticize him with words, if someone has done something wrong, lest an occasion be given for quarrels or hatred between citizens. They honor the faith given in the most sacred manner, and continue in their promises, leading the most wretched faith to be turned into treachery. But there is one exquisite virtue in which they excel the others: namely, the silence of those who are discussed in the senate. Their plans are very secret when the state of the state

is in question. For their decrees are covered with so much silence, that they appear at last, when the things which they had previously decreed are executed. For about eight months there was a debate in the senate about the removal of Carminiola, the leader of the war, which was never known until he was captured and punished for the error.

20. What can I say about their wonderful gratitude for the good they deserve from the republic? No one, if he has provided a benefit, who has not obtained the greatest benefits? How many because of their outstanding deeds to the country translated to aristocratic families? How many nobles did they acquire? This alone surpasses the rest of the cities which are in existence. This alone holds sway. This, the model of virtues, provides merit for a long time. This is a model of gratitude and a spur to virtue. What shall I say of the most honorable manners, which every age preserves intact and uncorrupted? Honesty of words prevails most. No eloquent insults, no base insults, no obscenity of words, no hateful controversies in conversation. Honesty of mouth and body is valued. They do not abuse each other.

21. That decorum prevails among them, especially praised by Cicero. But great reverence is paid to old age, in the manner of the Lacedaemonians, which is the best among them, that the elders should precede in honor, that a more dignified place may be given to those who have advanced in age. Adolescents are trained in the best education of life, so that they are brought up from their earliest years, so that they seem to be bred to modesty and honesty. No play is permitted to him in his age, except the care of letters or private business. They do a great deal of work in persuasive cases and are very much exercised in them. Those who are older in age are especially respected, yielding to the elders and bearing a certain gravity of life before them. At the beginning of this order of age, better men emerge from a well-behaved youth, and then emerge the best and modest old men. For there is no difficulty, no effort, to cultivate virtue for him who has been led from tender years to the path of honor. Aristotle writes to contribute much to the rest of the course of life by the learning and manners of his youth. For the former age, imbued with bad manners, and nourished by bad arts, was seldom wont to turn out into a good man or a good citizen.

22. Now, indeed, how much our religion flourishes among them, how much it is worshiped with honor, the adornment of the churches shows, the worship of God in the churches. There are many places of religious people, to which the citizens go for the purpose of prayer, distributing a great deal of grace for the use of the poor. They worship piety above all, and especially employ it

in preserving the citizens, if those who have been thrown more harshly by fortune lose their property, whom they do not depress or imprison, as is customary in most places, but they lift and support them, and encourage them to hope for a better fortune. For they think that the strength of the state is diminished if it is deserted by the citizens by some accidental calamity. It is also wonderful to see how much care and attention they take to attract the common people to live in the city, how they nurture and provide for the grain business by various practices, so that the common people do not lack anything, the less they can live comfortably in the city. The weaker ones are not harassed by any tribute, nor are they affected by any injury or calamity, by which things the city is always the most populous. But what is the highest bond of concord among the citizens, and the preservation of the city, is a diligent, fair, and modest method of contributing taxes, when the nobles contribute all taxes, not from the lust or discretion of the powerful, but according to the means of their means from the census. For they alone bear the burdens of the commonwealth, which the more they bear, the lighter they seem to each. For that weight is more easily borne, to which all lean with equal strength.

23. Therefore, whether war is to be waged by land or by sea, funds are readily available, and for want of them no occasion for the good administration of the matter is postponed more slowly than expediency demands. In this distribution of funds, not only Italy but all the nations of the world excel. Indeed, according to the custom of the ancient Romans, a census is taken, both of the citizens and of all their fortunes, which never ceases to contain the health of the state. For one is not emptied and the other enriched in time of war, as we see elsewhere, but there is an equal loss of all, as of one's patrimony. For this reason, they use the greatest care in deciding on wars, for they consult more often than they decide, and they are slow to consider the events of things earlier, for fear of expense and danger.

24. But the chief praise of the Venetians is that they render the upper sea safe from pirates, and do not allow that if any citizens are robbed by maritime robbers, that this is an unprovoked deed.

25. Nor, indeed, is there a greater concern for them to persecute robbers and pirates than to keep the citizens in their duty and to observe them at night. Father's son, son punishes father while in office for wrong quality. There is no room for intercession, no prayers, no friendship. Laws prevail, which no one transgresses. No one solves new laws or interprets them in their own sense. If anyone either embezzles the treasury, or exhausts the common fortunes, or

secretly steals anything from the public, or converts it into private property by some fraud, he is condemned to be punished severely. But this is a matter of great dishonor, that every year their names are publicly listed in the senate for perpetual disgrace, so that the notoriously infamous people are deterred from wrongdoing.

26. With these leaders, magistrates, laws, morals, institutions, and rules of government, the Venetians not only preserved their republic for more than seven hundred years, but gradually increased their empire by land and sea, so that their fame and virtue were celebrated throughout the whole world. Indeed, in the time of Charles the Great emperor, Maurice was the leader of the Venetians, whose son was captured by Desiderius, king of the Lombards, and the free work of Charles was restored to his father. I would not have denied, indeed I am certain, that there had been many Venetian leaders before Maurice. But it is quite a great praise and glory that one and the same form of governing the state has lasted for so many years, which has never happened to any state before. Considering the causes of this long-standing and long-lasting state of the republic, it strikes me that the most important justice is that Aristotle writes that the surest foundation of republics prevailed in that city before others, and that it was not men but laws that ruled in it. That virtue alone has made the republic of the Venetians firm, stable, and perpetual to this day. For there has never been a city, no kingdom, no republic where it has been more long, more severe, and more sincere, where equal honor has been held and spent on justice at such a time, where public laws have been more obeyed. It is also to be hoped, if anything can be long in human affairs, that this republic, so settled, so instituted, will be so far away from factions as to contend with eternity.

LATIN TEXT

ORATIO POGII FLORENTINI IN LAUDEM REIPUBLICAE VENETORUM.

SINGULAREM reipublicae Venetorum in omni virtutum genere praestantiam quibus possem laudibus prosequi cupientem, tum plurime ad hanc diem a scribendi studio atque ab rebus domesticis occupationes ab ea cura averterunt, tum timor quidam ne possem rerum dignitati parem dicendi facundiam praestare. Nunc vero maiori fretus ocio et simul animo versans fortes a fortuna adiuvari solitos, quod antea mente conceperam explicare litteris decrevi, ut et tam praeclara civitas meritis a nobis laudibus celebretur, et reliquae ad imitandas tam bene moratae reipublicae institutiones ex illarum memoria et laude incitentur. Nam si qua fuit usquam ullo unquam tempore respublica laude et gloria digna, si qua unquam iustitiae praecepta coluit, si qua bonis usa moribus gravitatem ac dignitatem tum in privatis tum in publicis negociis servavit, si qua extitit in qua communis utilitas privato commodo sit praelata, haec est una profecto, quae omnium quae sunt, quae fuerunt, quaeve sint futurae merito gloriam antecellat.

2. Variae sunt politiarum species, prout Aristoteli placet, quarum duas praefert caeteris, regnum scilicet et aristocratiam, quam nostri optimatum appellant, et eam Cicero in libris De Legibus optimam esse ait, quam viri optimi, ut ei placet, gubernant, laudi et gloriae servientes, conservatores patriae et reipublicae amatores. Talem profecto nunquam apud Venetos fuisse verissime affirmarim, apud quos soli optimates civitatem regunt, obtemperantes legibus intentique omnes ad publici status utilitatem, omni rei privatae cura posthabita. Hanc aristocratiam nusquam vidit neque fuisse legit Aristoteles. Nam si eam uspiam inspicere potuisset, in qua princeps tanquam caput reliquis dignitate praeest, legibus et ipse parens, optimates deinde, tanquam membra capiti haerentia, iustitiam veluti certum aurigam in agendis sequuntur, hanc procul dubio caeteris omnibus praetulisset. Nam in ea tanquam regis imaginem et optimates deinceps uno animo, una voce, in unam eandem conspirantes sententiam conspexisset, regnumque et aristocratiam in eadem republica contineri. Ex quo necesse est eam optimam omnium rempublicam arbitremur. Ipsemet fatetur Aristoteles satius esse a multis bonis quam ab uno regi. Itaque tanto videtur esse satius regnum ab optimatum republica superari, quanto maior, copiosior, amplior, uberior est, et usu melior multorum quam unius virtus, quantoque

magis diffunduntur inter mortales plurium beneficia quam unius, pluraque commoda importat secum multorum quam singularis viri probitas et sapientia. Haec etiam Lampridii in Vita Alexandri Severi est sententia. Ait enim: Notum est illud pietati tuae, quod in Mario Maximo legisti, meliorem esse rempublicam et prope tutiorem, in qua princeps malus est, ea in qua amici principis mali. Siquidem unus malus potest a pluribus bonis corrigi, multi autem mali non possunt ab uno quamvis bono ulla ratione superari. Qualis ergo ea respublica est dicenda, quae bono principi addit optimos consultores et multorum virtutem in unam contrahit voluntatem? Beatissima profecto atque omnium praestantissima existimanda est, et quam nusquam Aristoteles novit. Platonem quoque existimo, si hanc egregiam regendae civitatis formam perspicere potuisset, nullam aliam in sui operis exemplar fuisse positurum. Optimum enim statum reipublicae quaerebat, cuius fundamentum iustitiam designavit, ea cum praemio contineatur et poena ut boni viri virtutis praemio ad laudem incitentur, mali vero proposito facinorum supplicio a maleficiis deterreantur. Necesse est hanc illam esse quam philosophi quaesiverunt, quorum praeceptis ea respublica est constituta, in qua iustitia dominetur omnibus, per quam boni honorentur pro meritis, reprobi debita animadversione afficiantur.

3. Verum ut aliorum comparatione magis elucescat huius reipublicae in administranda iustitia virtus, priscorum veteres politias et eorum mores consideremus. Laudantur maxime Lacedemonii, qui septingentos ferme, ut aiunt, annos unicis legibus et nunquam mutatis moribus vixisse perhibentur. At in eis varia semper regendi conditio, et nunquam diutius in eodem statu pertinens civitas, et nunc regibus, nunc tyrannis subdita, nunc variis lacerata factionibus, nunc intestinis discordiis quassata, plane ostendit non beatam sed infelicissimam, non quietam sed turbulentam, non publicis commodis, sed privatis odiis deditam fuisse, et tandem post multas clades Romanorum subiit servitutem.

4. Atheniensium civitas quali republica usa fuerit Graecae testantur historiae. Plebis iudicium de singulis rebus erat, quodque scito plebis fiebat, ratum firmumque habebatur. Huius decretis concitato multitudinis impetu optimi prestantissimique viri urbe eiciebantur. Cives egregii plebis iudicio capite damnabantur. Summi imperatores aut extorres patria exilio aut carcere mulctabantur. Nunc regibus serviens, nunc tyrannorum crudelitati, nunc agitata plebis temeritate, ingratissima profecto civitas, quae suos bellorum duces pro rerum bene gestarum mercede variis affecit calamitatibus, semper aut

domesticis seditionibus aut externis bellis exagitata. Improbi praeferebantur bonis, mali ad reipublicae munera accessebantur. Itaque cita eorum libertas periit.

5. Thebanorum civitas simili pernitie defecit. Nunc potentioribus civibus nunc tyrannis obtemperans, nunc domesticis factionibus vexata, ut non rempublicam in ea sed contentionum temeritatem dicas fuisse.

6. Magnam Carthaginensium ac praepotentem rempublicam ferunt, ut quae annos ferme quadraginta cum populo Romano de imperio certarit. At legimus quam varie, quam crudeliter, quam barbare, quam truculenter fuerit administrata: suos certe imperatores excellentissimos viros aut crudelissima morte affecit, aut proscripsit, ut potius superba atque impotens tyrannis sit quam respublica nominanda.

7. Maxima omnium quae unquam fuerunt Romana respublica fuit summisque laudibus celebrata. Eloquentia et dicendi copia vel vicit vel equavit omnes. Virtute bellica superavit. Multi in ea in omni laudis genere viri optimi praeclarissimique floruerunt. Sed quis nescit quot quantique in ea civitate ab ipso libertatis initio novi motus, quantae rerum varietates, quantae turbines, quantae dissentiones, discidia, seditiones in mobili populo viguerunt quot quantaque patriae et plebis certamina sunt excitata, quae patrum et consulum cum tribunis plebis concertationes ? redscidia, odia, bella plusquam civilia, furta, rapinae, proscriptiones civium, optimorum virorum exilia, turbulentiae demum innumerabilis exortae, ceu cum tempestuosum mare continuis fluctibus agitaretur. Non recenseo consulum, praetorum, caeterorumque magistratuum spolia, sacrilegia, stupra, caedes, urbium desolationes, militum libidinem et avaritiam. Praetermitto pessimam in subditos tyrannidem, nefaria scelera in provinciis maiorum infanda libidine patrata. Cicero ipse testatur plures sociorum civitates hibernis militum, quam eorum armis hostium urbes fuisse deletas. Taceo varias coniurationes contra rempublicam excitatas et orbem terrarum Romanorum avaritiae concessum. Quid referam Verres, Clodios, Catilinas, aliosque conspirantes in provinciarum et urbis perniciem procreatos? Illud verissime videor posse dicere: multis seculis non rempublicam sed nefarium latrocinium saevissimamque tyrannidem appellari potuisse, cum neque leges, neque mores et instituta maiorum, neque iudicia valerent, sed vis, ferrum, cedes in foro et deorum templis tribunorum conspiratione versarentur. Ipse Cicero queritur nullam esse rempublicam, nulla iudicia, nullum senatum, sed Pompeii nutu omnia in contrarium agi. Fuit apud priscos Romanos

aliquando tempus quo respublica dici mereretur, sed tunc quoque plebis secessio, decemvirum libido, Coriolani Cammilique exilia recenseri possunt.

8. At vero Venetorum respublica longe a superiorum consuetudine remota, omnibus his caruit vitiis ac flagitiis, quibus caeterae civitates et respublicae conciderunt. Nullae inter ipsos in administranda republica discordiae, nulla dissensio, nullae civium contentiones, nullae factiones, nullae simultates, nulla aperta odia. Idem sentiunt singuli unoque omnes animo ad reipublicae salutem concurrunt. Ad hanc mentem dirigunt, in ea tuenda totis viribus incumbunt. Id quaerunt, id appetunt, ut eorum respublica sit quam beatissima. Hoc quamvis arduum in civitate tanta existimetur, nequaquam tamen mirum cuipiam debet videri, si modum regendae urbis recognoscant. Sunt enim familiae perantiquae ac nobiles permultae, in quibus reipublicae gubernatio continetur. Nulli plebeo aditus aut locus datur ad munia civitatis. Sole nobilitati et ex ea viris praestantioribus publica demandantur officia, quo fit ut singuli, velut unius eiusdemque corporis membra ad illius salutem ac valitudinem unica voluntate concurrant, et tanquam propriam matrem sibi fovendam ac nutriendam putent. Merito igitur hanc rempublicam caeteris longo intervallo virtute anteire putandum est, cuius rei ut maximum id est argumentum, quod ultra septingentesimum annum, quod nulla alia in republica contigit, eisdem duce, magistratibus, legibus, institutis, moribus ad hanc diem perseveravit.

9. Sed in tam amplae, tam magnificae civitatis laudibus, primum, quod multum existimo ad laudem et gloriam urbis conferre, situs eius occurit, de quibus dicendum esse videatur. Edificata est eo loci civitas, ut quamvis nullis cincta moenibus, nullis propungnaculis munita tamen sit omnium tutissima, nullas machinas, nulla instrumenta bellica expavescat, nullos subitos impetus, nullos improvisos incursus hostium reformidet. Mari undequaque cincta externo vacat metu. Nam et ab continenti quinque distat miliaribus, quibus veluti fossa aggere circumdata navigant, ut nihil sit ab ea parte extimescendum. Et unico tam en ornata est portu, quo maioribus navibus, si sint onustae, non datur accessus, et triremibus caeterisque navigiis omnem hostilem classem parvo labore aditu arcere quaeat. Nam reliquis in locis stagnantes et veluti palustres aquae haud magnis sunt navibus perviae. Ita nullae equitum excursiones, nullae sunt hostiles classes pertimescendae. Murus est praeterea ex congestis lapidibus latissimus xx milium passuum, defixis ingentibus palis stabilis, qui vim maris fluentis arceat a civitate et loca stagnantia dat tranquilliora.

10. Quod vero mirabile est dictu et civitati praecipuum decus praebet atque ornamentum, navalia existunt amplissima ac magnifico apparatu, quibus caetera orbis longe sunt postponenda, ad quorum conservationem certa sunt vectigalia instituta. In iis amplius centum triremes ociosae, suis armamentis paratae, ut de his quae in usu sunt mercaturae sileatur, et onerariae naves permultae, ut infra mensem si opus sit, centum quinquaginta maiorum navium paratam classem atque instructam educere extra portum quaeant. Nam reliquarum minorum infinita paene est multitudo. Maximus est enim numerus earum, quae ad vehendum usui necessaria sunt accommodata. Omnia quippe ad victum oportuna tantae urbi alendae mari abunde deferuntur, ut semper ibi sit rerum omnium copia, neque ulla inopia timeatur. Pulcherrimum praebent spectaculum naves permultae aut venientes aut abeuntes, tum quae ad propriora pergunt loca, tum quae in Pontum et Meotidas navigant paludes caeterosque infidelium portus, tum quae Hispaniam, Galliam, Britanniam, et Morinos petunt mercaturae gratia. Hae omnes variis rebus oneratae cum eunt maximum spectaculum urbi praebent. Inde ad Mediterranea loca ad alias regiones, alias provincias curribus, omnis generis mercatura defertur.

11. Quid referam pulcherrimas domos, magnifica palatia, templa magno sumptu aedificata, plateas et publica loca ac civitatem variis artificibus refertam? Quid recenseam adolescentum modestiam, auctoritatem senum, gravitatem virorum, senatus dignitatem, qui verissime ex regibus, ut olim Cineas de Romanis dixit, videtur constare? Quid civium omnium dignitatem quandam prae se ferentium ornatum vestium? Quid variam mundamque supellectilem, in cuius ornamentum plurimam impendunt curam? Adde quod urbs omnis tum stratis viis tum canalibus est pervia, quae magna est et haud parvi commoditas facienda. Singula enim quae ad victum spectant domum usque naviculis deferuntur. In quo vero plurimum extollendi sunt, amplitudo est decorque ecclesiarum, quas variis rebus exornant ad cultum religionis. Sed haec cum multis aliis communia existunt. In quo vero caeteros excedunt, opulentia est et thesaurus templi Sancti Marci, quod quidem ipsum est ornatissimum et aspectu mirabile: magna vis est auri atque argenti, margaritarum quoque et eorum quos lapides vulgus appellat praetiosos, quos et exquisitos et plurimi pretii affirmant.

12. Quoniam vero ordine et ratione singula reguntur et perficiuntur, quae mihi secundo loco proposui dicenda, ordo ipse magistratuum, quibus commissa est reipublicae gubernandae cura, ab ipsius urbis initio institutis paucis recensebo. Ducem in urbis principio sibi crearunt cives, qui tanquam

caput praeesset omnibus ac publicae consuleret utilitati, et ipse legibus subditus, ut cum fit superior dignitate, legibus obtemperandis par reliquis existat. Neque enim si deliquerit poenam subterfugit, sed a magistratu punitur ex legum institutis. Huic soli nulla potestas concessa. Ita praeest caeteris ut nihil solus possit decernere quod ad rempublicam pertineat, non litteras scribere, non reserare allatas, non audire quemquam, non respondere nisi de voluntate sex virorum, quorum consilio haerere debet. Horum suprema potestas est et legibus subdita. Hic eligitur suffragio senatus, eiusdemque iudicio, siquando opus fuerit, amovetur, sed ferme omnes in ea dignitate moriuntur. Iudicio tamen subest, siquid commiserit quod graviori egeat censura. Ut autem constet quantum insita sit mentibus singulorum aequi bonique cultus, quanta modestia duces vixerint, nemo dicitur in tot seculorum curriculis ad tyrannidem aspirasse praeter unum qui et temeritatis suae poenas dedit, quod hercle mirandum videtur, cum tam potens morbus in hominibus sit ambitio, tanta cupiditas dominandi. Sed patriae caritas omnes apud eos exuperat animi passiones. Omnes expellit insanas cupiditates. Sciunt praeterea se legum custodes esse, non dominos. Sciunt curam regendae civitatis una cum reliquis, non imperium demandatum.

13. Id praecipue maxima laude extollendum, quod eorum leges firmae sunt, stabiles longaevaeque quoad reipublicae utilitas ferat, neque pro voluntate cuiusquam abrogantur, neque variantur in diem, sed perpetua sanctione custodiuntur. Sunt praeter hos, quos recensui, decem viri in annum creati ex primariis civitatis, quibus sontes scelestosque ex quavis causa pro qualitate facinorum puniendi proscribendique potestas est attributa , a quorum sententia nulla datur provocatio neque quod egerint retractare fas est. Iuri reddendo suus est magistratus, a quo aguntur civium ac peregrinorum causae, non libellis tabellionum, non iurisconsultorum callida interpretatione, sed aequitate, modestia, ratione, in quibus parva tum impensa, tum iactura temporis consumitur. Neque vero in iure reddendo aut iustitia quovismodo administranda ullo externo utuntur ministro, sed ipsimet ex ordine magistratuum ius dicunt ea moderatione ut aut nullae aut rarae querelae ex eorum iudiciis fiant.

14. Adduntur his templi Sancti Marci, ut appellant, procuratores, viri electi ex omnibus, dignitate et auctoritate graves, quorum munus est tueri thesaurum templi dispensareque in pios usus quod superest ab illius religionis cultu et ornatu. Sunt quoque et officiales, ut dicunt, noctis, quibus cura

imminet minora delicta pro eorum qualitate castigandi, et ea praesertim quae nocturno tempore committuntur.

15. Est praeterea minor senatus ducentorum hominum institutus, quem vocant rogatos, in quem omnes conveniunt, quos supra retuli magistratus. In hoc conventu dux praeest excelsiori sedens loco, postque eum reliqui sequuntur pro singulorum dignitate. Ibi quae ad statum civitatis quaeve ad bellum aut pacem pertinent, discussis sententiis decernuntur. Adiicitur cum causa postulat alter senatus numeri amplioris, cum singulis nobilibus, modo vigesimum excedant annum, datur interesse. Horum suffragiis singuli creantur praetores caeterique officiales, quibus exteriores provinciae, civitates, oppida regenda impartiuntur, aut aliquod imponitur speciale munus. Est omnibus huius coetus, quibus id forte contigit, quos velint pro arbitrio eligendi nominandique libera facultas. Qui ex nominatis per senatus suffragium eligitur, dat certam, ut leges iubent, mercedem ei qui se nominavit. Qua ex re duo virtutis praemia oriuntur: primum eius qui dignum magistratu virum nominat, tum vero nominati, si fuerit designatus. Ita virtutis contentio est atque aemulatio inter cives, non odii aut temeritatis. Quilibet enim nititur ut talis evadat moribus ad hominum famam et opinionem, ut suffragiis caeteros antecellat. Ea neque precibus impediuntur neque ambitione, quo fit ut optimo cuique aditus pateat ad dignitates. Singuli enim laudem sibi peperisse putant si talem nominarint, qui dignus ea dignitate senatus iudicio existimetur.

16. Memini quosdam magna poena mulctatos, qui in dendis suffragiis pro amico intercessisse precibus dicebantur. Volunt enim liberas esse hominum voluntates in rebuspublicis, non pretio aut precibus emptas. Quapropter raro deputantur ad imperandum aliis nisi quorum virtutem cognitam et perspectam habent. Quodsi qui in subditos aut avarius aut crudelius quam lege liceat se gerant, severe puniuntur. Audiuntur enim oppressorum querelae et ab iniuriis vindicantur. Ideo manus continent ab iniuriis puras, et tantum agunt quantum leges sinant, quae omnes spectant ad iustitiae cultum.

17. Hoc vivendi instituto, his moribus, hoc ordine, nullo unquam tempore posteaquam coepit intermissio, adeo iuste sancteque gubernatur civitas, adeo aequa omnibus in suo gradu potestas, adeo par viris honorumque distributio, ut non humanis consiliis sed divino quodam nutu, non terrena sed aliqua celesti monarchia tanta civitas, tam concordi civium voluntate regi et conservari videatur. Id enim cogitant, id quaerunt, ad id attendunt singuli, quod arbitrantur reipublicae profuturum. Quod siquando, ut accidit, cum aut de bello aut de pace agendum est, variae fuerint civium sententiae et inter se

diversae, quod maior pars decreverit id reliqui comprobant et sequuntur, opinionemque suam, etiam si secus senserint, in alterius sententiam traducunt. Nulla perstat voluntatum obstinatio, nullum odium, nulla simultas rempublicam labefactat. Facile se vinci in sua sententia patiuntur. Ita diversitas opinionum in concordiam redacta. Nulla pactione aut conspiratione civium retractatur.

18. Hoc pacto unam omnium mentem, unam voluntatem, unum animum, unicum consilium diceres extitisse. Nulla domus privata in qua sit pater familias non insulsus, nulli fratres, nulli affines tam communi, tam concordi animo privatum commodum quaerunt, quanto Veneti suae urbis statum et dignitatem. Nemo de sua re in consulendo cogitat, sed communem ante oculos utilitatem propositam intuetur. Id vero praecipue summa laus ducenda: si qui pro commisso maleficio sint damnandi, e vestigio si fuerint comprehensi scelerum poenas luunt. Nulla datur intercessio, nulla remissio, nullum subterfugium, nullius interventu cursus iustitiae impeditur. Rarissime revocantur exules nisi exacta poena. Et cum sint severi iustitiae exactores, tamen ea est admirabilis civium prudentia. Nam si quis suo merito reipublicae muneribus privetur, aut ex urbe eiciatur, aut puniatur capite. Eius solius qui deliquerit poena contenti. Caeteros eiusdem stirpis sive domus, aut filios, aut cognatos ut innoxios sinunt eligi ad magistratus, adesse consiliis, venire in senatum, reipublicae munera exercere. Relegatur persaepe pater, priorem in urbe statum locumque filio conservante, ut, secundum propheticam sententiam, anima quae peccaverit, ipsa moriatur. Soli ibi sontes plectantur; caeteris status integer republica preservatur.

19. Neque vero licet cuiquam alterius exprobare errata aut verbis insectari, si quis quid deliquerit, ne detur occasio ad iurgia vel odia inter cives ferenda. Fidem datam colunt sanctissime inque promissis perstant, turpissimum ducentes fidem in perfidiam verti. Una vero et ea exquisita virtus, in qua caeteris antecellant: taciturnitas videlicet eorum, quae in senatu tractantur. Sunt eorum consilia secretissima, cum de statu agitur civitatis. Tanto enim silentio eorum decreta teguntur, ut tum denique appareant, cum executio fiat rerum, quas antea decrevere. Octo fere mensibus est in senatu de tollendo duce belli Carminiola agitatum, id nunquam scitum est priusquam is captus erroris poenas dedit.

20. Quid dicam illorum miram in bene merentes de republica gratitudinem? Nullus, si beneficium praestitit, qui non fuerit amplissima beneficia assecutus? Quot ob eorum egregia erga patriam facinora ad

optimatum familias traduxerunt? Quot nobilium numero asciverunt? Haec una caeteras urbes quae sunt quaeve fuere sola superat. Haec sola principatum obtinet. Haec, virtutum specimen, merita diu praebet. Haec gratitudinis exemplar et ad virtutes aculeus. Quid loquar de moribus honestissimis, quos omnis aetas integros servat atque incorruptos? Verborum honestas viget maxima. Nullae dicaces contumeliae, nulla turpia convicia, nulla verborum obscenitas, nullae odiosae in colloquendo concertationes. Honestas oris et corporis habetur in pretio. Nullis invicem contumeliis agitantur.

21. Decorum illud inter eos viget, a Cicerone maxime laudatum. Senectuti vero magna adhibetur reverentia, Lacedemoniorum more, qui est apud eos optimus, ut seniores honore praecedant, ut iis dignior tribuatur locus, qui aetate antecesserint. Adolescentes optima vitae institutione erudiuntur, ita ut a primis annis educati, ut ad modestiam et honestatem procreati esse videantur. Nullus ludus ei conceditur aetati praeterquam litterarum aut privatorum negociorum curam. Magnam in perorandis causis operam praestant inque his plurimum exercentur. Superiores aetate reverentur praecipue, cedentes maioribus et vitae quandam gravitatem prae se ferentes. Hoc ineuntis aetatis ordine, ex bene acta adolescentia meliores emergunt viri, inde optimi modestique evadunt senes. Nulla est enim difficultas, nullus labor virtutem colere ei, qui sit a teneris annis ad honesti viam traductus. Multum conferre scribit Aristoteles ad reliquum vitae cursum qua eruditione, quibus moribus fuerit adolescentiae iter institutum. Raro enim prior aetas, malis imbuta moribus, malis enutrita artibus in virum bonum aut probum civem evadere consuevit.

22. Iam vero nostra religio quanta apud eos vigeat, quanto colatur honore, ornatus templorum ostendit, ecclesiarum cultus. Religiosorum loca sunt permulta, ad quae cives adeunt orandi causa, gratia plurima in usum pauperum distribuentes. Pietatem maxime colunt, eamque praecipue adhibent in conservandis civibus, si qui a fortuna asperius iactati rem suam amisere, quos non deprimunt aut in carcerem trudunt, ut pluribus in locis consuevit, sed sublevant ac sustentant hortanturque ad spem fortunae melioris. Minui enim vires civitatis putant, si deseratur a civibus aliqua tempestate fortuita calamitosis. Mirum est etiam cernere quanta cura atque diligentia alliciant plebem ad habitandum in urbe, quam variis exercitiis nutriunt ac provident rei frumentariae, ne quid popularibus desit, quo minus in civitate esse commode possint. Nullo tributo vexantur tenuiores, nulla iniuria afficiuntur aut calamitate, quibus rebus civitas est semper populosissima. Quod vero est

civium summum concordiae vinculum et urbis conservatio, est tributi conferendi diligens, aequa et modesta ratio, cum non ex libidine aut arbitrio potentiorum, sed pro modo facultatum ex censu optimates omnes tributa conferant. Iis enim solis sunt civitatis onera subeunda, quae quo plures ferunt, eo videntur esse singulis leviora. Illud enim pondus facilius fertur, ad quod omnes aequis viribus incumbunt.

23. Itaque sive terra sive mari bellum sit gerendum, in promptu sunt pecuniae, neque earum inopia ulla bene administrandae rei occasio tardius quam utilitas postulat differtur. Qua in distributione sumptuum, non solum Italiae sed omnes orbis nationibus excellunt. More siquidem priscorum Romanorum census fit et civium et eorum omnium fortunarum, qui mos nunquam intermissus salutem continet civitatis. Non enim unus exinanitur alter ditatur belli tempore, prout alibi fieri videmus, sed aequa omnium tanquam unius patrimonii fit iactura. Ea re in decernendis bellis summam adhibent diligentiam, consultant enim saepius quam decernunt, suntque ad deliberandum impensarum et periculi metu tardiores rerum eventa maturius pensitantes.

24. Praecipua vero Venetorum est laus, quod superum mare tutum a piratis praestant, neque sinunt, si qui cives a maritimis praedonibus spolientur, id facinus inultum esse, sed armata classe illos quocumque iverint, quoad capti afficiantur poena vel rapta restituantur.

25. Neque vero maior imminet eis cura praedones et piratas persequendi quam continendi in officio cives et in sontes animadvertendi. Filium pater, patrem filius dum est in magistratu pro errati qualitate castigat. Non intercessioni, non precibus, non amicitiae locus deprecandi est ullus. Leges dominantur, quas nemo transgitur. Nemo novas solvit leges aut in suum sensum interpretatur. Si quis aut aerarium expilarit, aut communes fortunas exhauserit aut quicquam occulte subripuerit ex publico aut in privatam rem fraude aliqua converterit, e vestigio damnatus acri poena afficitur. Id vero magno dedecori est, quod annis singulis ad perpetuam ignominiam publice in senatu recensentur eorum nomina, ut tantae infamiae nota caeteii a maleficio deterreantur.

26. His duce, magistratibus, legibus, moribus, institutis et regendi norma, ultra septingentos annos Veneti eorum rempublicam non conservarunt solum, sed indies eorum imperium terra marique auxerunt, ut per universum orbem illorum fama virtusque celebretur. Caroli siquidem Magni imperatoris tempore, Mauritius dux erat Venetorum, cuius filius a Desiderio

PRAISE FOR THE REPUBLIC OF VENICE

Longobardorum rege captus opera Caroli liber restituitur patri. Non negaverim, immo certus sum, et ante Mauritium plures fuisse Venetorum duces. Sed satis magna laus et gloria est unam et eandem regendae civitatis formam tot iugiter annos, quod nulli unquam antea civitati contigit, perdurasse. Huius tam longaevi tamque diuturni reipublicae status causas consideranti mihi illa occurrit potissima iustitiam quam scribit Aristoteles rerumpublicarum certissimum fundamentum in ea urbe prae caeteris viguisse, neque homines sed leges in ea imperasse. Ea sola virtus ad hanc diem firmam, stabilem, perpetuam praestitit rempublicam Venetorum. Nulla enim unquam fuit civitas, nullum regnum, nulla respublica ubi diutius, severius, sincerius fuerit versata, ubi par honor tanto tempore iustitiae fuerit habitus et impensus, ubi magis fuerit legibus publicis obtemperatum. Sperandum quoque est, si quid diu in humanis rebus esse potest, hanc rempublicam ita moratam, ita institutam, factiones tantummodo absint, cum aeternitate esse certaturam.

The Scriptorium Project is the work of a small group of lay people of various apostolic churches who are interested in the preservation, transmission, and translation of the works of the early and medieval church. Our efforts are to make the works of the church fathers accessible to anyone who might have an interest in Christian antiquities and the theological, philosophical, and moral writings that have become the bedrock of Western Civilization.

To-date, our releases have pulled from the Greek, Syriac, Georgian, Latin, Celtic, Ethiopian, and Coptic traditions of Christianity, and have been pulled from sundry local traditions and languages.

www.ingramcontent.com/pod-product-compliance
Lightning Source LLC
LaVergne TN
LVHW052049070526
838201LV00086B/5164